Little Sisters,
LiSteN up!

Also from the Boys Town Press

Who's Raising Your Child?
Common Sense Parenting®
Parenting to Build Character in Your Teen
Common Sense Parenting of Toddlers and Preschoolers
Common Sense Parenting Learn-at-Home Video or DVD Kit
Angry Kids, Frustrated Parents
Dealing with Your Kids' 7 Biggest Troubles
Parents and Kids Talking About School Violence
Practical Tools for Foster Parents
Safe and Effective Secondary Schools
Teaching Social Skills to Youth
The Well-Managed Classroom
Unmasking Sexual Con Games
The Ongoing Journey
Journey of Faith
Journey of Hope
Journey of Love

For Adolescents

Boundaries: A Guide for Teens
A Good Friend
Who's in the Mirror?
What's Right for Me?

For a free Boys Town Press catalog, call 1-800-282-6657
Visit our web site at www.boystownpress.org

Little Sisters, ListeN Up!

A Message of Hope
for Girls Growing Up in Poverty, Racism, and Despair

by
Ruby Asugha, M.A., M.M.

BOYS TOWN, NEBRASKA

Little Sisters, Listen Up!
Published by the Boys Town Press
Father Flanagan's Boys' Home
Boys Town, NE 68010

Copyright © 2004, by Father Flanagan's Boys' Home

ISBN 1-889322-61-X

The Boys Town Press is the publishing division of Girls and Boys Town, the original Father Flanagan's Boys' Home.

Publishers' Cataloging-in-Publication Data

Asugha, Ruby.

    Little sisters, listen up! : a message of hope to girls growing up in poverty, racism, and despair / Ruby Asugha. -- 1st ed. -- Boys Town, Neb. : Boys Town Press, 2004.

        p. ; cm.

    ISBN: 1-889322-61-X

    1. Self-actualization (Psychology) in adolescence--United States. 2. Self-esteem in adolescence--United States. 3. Self-perception in adolescence--United States. 4. Race awareness in adolescence--United States. 5. African American teenage girls--Life skills guides. 6. Teenage girls--United States--Life skills guides. 7. Poor youth--United States--Life skills guides. 8. Oppression (Psychology) I. Title.

BF637.S4 A88 2004
158.1/084/22--dc22   0407

10 9 8 7 6 5 4 3 2 1

Table of Contents

Introduction
Three Friends 3

Chapter 1
Love 19

Chapter 2
Poverty 31

Chapter 3
Racism 39

Chapter 4
Worthlessness 51

Chapter 5
The American Dream 59

Chapter 6
Pressure 67

Chapter 7
Faith and Spirituality 77

Chapter 8
Self-Esteem 85

Chapter 9
Loneliness 93

Chapter 10
Pain and Pleasure 105

Chapter 11
Role Models 117

Chapter 12
Purpose 127

Chapter 13
Listen Up, Little Sisters 137

"It is the mind that rules the body."

Sojourner Truth
Evangelist and Reformer
(1797 – 1883)

This African American woman was born Isabella Baumfree, the daughter of slaves, and spent her childhood as an abused slave of several masters. When the state of New York abolished slavery in 1828, Sojourner Truth (the name she gave herself) traveled the country preaching and fighting to end slavery nationwide and to gain rights for women. Her courage in the face of tremendous adversity continues to inspire many African Americans.

Three Friends

Ruby

"Hello little sisters, my name is Ruby and I'm a lot like you. I was born in Chicago – the west side of town. I grew up in a two-family flat building. My grandmother lived on the first floor. The second floor was home to my father, a pastor; my mother, a saint in my eyes; and my three brothers and five sisters. I'm the youngest.

"Most of the buildings around me were dilapidated and some were literally crumbling to the ground. If you walked out onto the back porch of one of these buildings, you would have fallen through to the ground. I had friends who lived in these decaying buildings. Outside my door, on street corners, there were drug dealers, gang members, and hookers drinking booze, smoking, getting high. Day and night, the air was filled with the sounds of gunshots, police and ambulance sirens, yelling and screaming from arguments and fights. It just never seemed to stop. Violence and gangs, alcohol and drugs, sex and prostitution – it was everywhere. Chaos reigned supreme; there was no place outside to escape it.

"I remember sometimes being scared to death to walk to school or go to the store on the corner, even during the day! When I'd go places, I always went with a group of other kids. That way, it was less likely that one of us would get robbed or raped. My sister was pretty smart and she would dress like she was crazy so the scary men would leave her alone. I was lucky, blessed really, that I had a mother and a father who loved, cared, and watched out for me."

'Shawna'

"Some of my girlfriends didn't have both parents in their household. One of my good friends, Shawna, lived right across the street in a three-story building. I could see her from my window, and we'd wave to each other. She was the oldest of eight kids.

"Shawna's mom didn't work and was on welfare. Shawna was expected to help cook, clean, and take care of her little brothers and sisters. Sometimes she had to miss school to do these things, but Shawna's mother didn't care about that. She was more concerned about satisfying her own immediate needs, which meant buying and using alcohol and cigarettes. Shawna was determined not to end up like her mother. She wanted to get an education and a good job, and live in a nice house. She wanted to get out of the ghetto in the worse way. We grew close, studied together, and worked hard on our homework.

"Shortly after high school, Shawna met a man and thought she was in love. He gave her all sorts of nice things and promised her a great life filled with love. Shawna was tired of the pressures and struggles inside her household and the violence outside it. To make matters worse, Shawna's brothers were involved with gang activity, drugs, and guns. So she left home to live with this man. Soon she was pregnant. The man left Shawna and the baby, and Shawna was left with broken dreams. Last I heard she joined the Army. This was her way out."

'Teah'

"My best friend growing up was Teah. We lived in the same neighborhood. Teah had three sisters, and they all lived together with their mother and stepfather. We went to the same high school and pushed each other real hard to do our best in school and other activities.

"In the seventh grade, our parents sacrificed many things so that we could go on a field trip to Disney World. When Teah and I got there, we thought we were in paradise – there was no violence or drugs or frightening people. Everything was so beautiful and serene. The grass was green and freshly mowed. The trees were tall and shapely. The daytime was filled with laughter and fun and the nights were calm and quiet. It was the most amazing time in our lives. Teah and I made a pact that, together, we would get out of the ghetto, go to college, and work at Disney World.

"In our junior year of high school, Teah hooked up with a guy whom she fell madly in love with. He had a nice car and an apartment filled with top-of-the-line furniture, a stereo, a TV – you name it and he probably had it. At the end of our junior year, I had earned enough school credits to graduate from high school. After graduating, I went off to college, and the plan was for Teah to join me the next year.

"When I came back after my first year in college, Teah had left home and moved in with the man of her dreams. He gave Teah jewelry and bought her very nice things. He told her that he loved her very much and couldn't live without her. Teah was the envy of many girls. But soon she got pregnant. Teah had an abortion, but the procedure went terribly wrong and she got very sick. More surgery was needed and, as a result, Teah wasn't able to have kids anymore. This man introduced Teah to drugs and the street life. She helped him make money by faking car accidents and getting hurt. He used the money to pay for drugs and all the nice things he had.

"Teah never joined me in college like we had planned for all those years. Eventually, the man left Teah, who was hooked on drugs. Last time I saw her, Teah was still living on the west side of Chicago. She looked decades older than she really was. Teah was a drug addict. She never made it out."

* * *

I suppose now you're wondering what happened to me. I graduated from college and went on to graduate school. Today, I have a good job at Girls and Boys Town where I help troubled kids. I have a loving husband, a great son, and a comfortable home. My brothers, sisters, and other family members remain important people in my life, and I'm an active member of a fantastic church. I have a wonderful life! I made it out.

That's my story, and it's all true. It's a story that's probably pretty similar to yours. Shawna, Teah, and I are really not any different than you and your friends. The main difference in my case is that I made it out and reached my goals and dreams. And you can too! But you have got to want it – and I mean you have to want it real bad!

You're going to face many tough choices and decisions every day. You're going to be tempted and pressured by others to escape it all by getting sucked into bad things like alcohol, drugs, and sex. And, you are going to have to overcome some wrong ways of thinking about yourself and your situation. It won't be easy. But you can do it! I know you can because I did.

My heartfelt hope is that you don't end up like my two friends. I'll always love them and I miss them very much, even today. But they made bad decisions and choices. They gave into the pressures and influences of the crowd, and they believed the faulty thinking that causes lots of African American teenage girls to end up in the same kinds of bad situations – pregnant and forced to turn to the government for a handout or living in a way that batters the body, mind, and spirit.

This kind of life is not your destiny. You do NOT have to end up this way. You can make it out and succeed. I won't kid you; there are going to be huge obstacles to overcome. I know that because I had to climb over many to succeed. So little sisters, listen up! I've got some things to tell you that I know will help you reach your goals and dreams.

In this book, I'll explain why a lot of African American teenage girls think the way they do and why this way of thinking is wrong. I'll talk about making choices and decisions, how bad ones are made, and why making good ones is so important. Also, I'll talk to you about why many African American girls end up the way they do.

It's important for you to understand all this because education is an important ingredient to changing your life and success. Without it, you can head in the wrong direction without even realizing it's happening.

I'm also going to talk about solutions – how you can make it out and be successful. These are lessons that I have learned on my journey out of the ghetto.

Girls, I care about you. There are lots of people who love and care about you. We hope and pray for you every day. I care so much that I want to share with you what I know and what I've learned along the way.

Experience is one of the best teachers. Trust me on this one; I had to learn it the hard way. So listen up to one of the voices of experience. I want to reach out and help any little sister who has goals and dreams and needs a little advice on how to make them a reality – just as I did.

Growing Up as an African American Girl

Okay little sisters, let's talk about some topics that are in your face every day. I'm talking about things like love, loneliness, poverty, racism, pressure, and others. These issues are complicated and confusing to young people. And you might think of them as obstacles or reasons why you can't reach your goals and dreams.

You have probably already formed ideas about what these things mean to you and how they affect your daily life. What I've found is that many of you have been taught the wrong information. This didn't happen on purpose. You learned it from the people around you – or the culture you grew up in. When a culture is not a positive and caring one, it has a negative effect on your attitudes, thinking, and actions. Over time, you start making bad choices and begin to lose hope.

What I'm concerned about is that you have the right information and understand the best ways to deal with these day-to-day issues. When you face them, I want you to be educated so that you're able to make good choices and decisions. Every day that you are able to do this gets you one step closer to success, whatever that means for you. Most of all, every time you make a good choice and experience success – no matter how small or insignificant it might seem – you keep hope alive.

Becoming a Better Person

Before we move on to the topics in this book, let's take a minute to talk about something I find to be very important: striving to become a better person. Why is this so important? Simply put, the choices you make today will affect your future, either positively or negatively. If your desire is to become a better daughter, sister, student, or friend, you're on the right path to enjoy all the good things that life has to offer. If you choose not to grow and get better as a person, then you're likely to get caught up in gangs, alcohol and drugs, and sex.

How do you go about becoming a better person? Well, little sisters, I'm going to give this one to you straight: You aren't going to achieve this goal unless you are self-motivated. This means being and staying determined and persevering even when there are no visible rewards for the things you do. It means that you take action and do things you might not always like or want to do because you want to succeed.

Let me show you what I mean with an example from just one part of your life. At your age, going to school and getting an education are the most important things you do every day to help yourself succeed. Self-motivation and school can be broken down into simple steps. First, you have to get out of bed when your alarm clock rings. Next, you have to get ready for school. Then, you have to get to school on time and be ready to learn. You see, little sisters, being self-motivated isn't some kind of magic dust that's sprinkled on you. It's all about taking one small step after another.

There are lots of times when you will not feel like going to school, or when you'll be having negative thoughts about what lies ahead in your school day. This is the time when you have to take action – little baby steps. It means that you do the next right thing, even though you might not want to.

When you commit to doing these small actions every day and then actually do them, they eventually become habits. These habits then become part of you, and doing the actions gets easier and easier over time.

If you apply this to other parts of your life, you'll find another great thing happening to you. As you do what you're supposed to do in all areas each day, good things will come from it. You'll start to feel good about yourself. You will have a sense of accomplishment, and your self-confidence will grow. You will believe in yourself and begin doing the right thing simply because it is the right thing to do. Before you know it, you'll want to do even more.

For example, when you do well and graduate from high school, you might decide to move on to college. When you do well and graduate from college, you might decide to move on and get a good job. When you do well in your job, you might want a better job. This wonderful cycle of success continues on and on until you find yourself doing and achieving more than you ever thought you would!

This "success cycle" can start with one task that's as simple as getting out of bed each and every morning. Then, it's up to you to take the next right step.

So, little sisters, just keep putting one foot in front of the other. Soon you'll be enjoying the success that comes from striving to be a better person and you'll find yourself moving on to bigger and better things!

Let's Go!

Okay, little sisters, let's begin setting the record straight. Let's bring these topics out in the open and discuss what girls your age think. I want to give you good information about these topics, information that I have learned from my experience. And, I want to give you some new ways of thinking and dealing with these issues so that you can overcome them, become a better person, and succeed.

You can also learn a lot from looking at examples of african american women who have overcome huge obstacles to make their dreams come true. Each chapter in this book begins with a quote from one of these women that I hope will inspire you. Some of these women you may recognize and some you may not. There is a short biography for you to read, but I also encourage you to go out and read more about them. They have played important roles in our culture and have helped to pave the way for other African Americans to succeed.

At the end of each chapter, there are some questions that will help you think about what these issues mean to you. Spend some time to consider them or discuss them with your friends or a trusted adult. Then write down your thoughts in the space provided. When you finish the book, you will have a personal plan of action for your own life – starting now!

"Just don't give up
trying to do what you
really want to do.
Where there's love and
inspiration, I don't
think you can go wrong."

Ella Fitzgerald
Jazz Singer
(1917 – 1996)

Born into poverty, Ella Fitzgerald was a teenager
when her mother died, and she was sent to live in
an orphanage. For a time, she was homeless. She was
blessed with a brilliant and beautiful voice that was
discovered when she won a contest at Harlem's
Apollo Theater. Fitzgerald worked hard and became
a world-famous jazz singer who won 12 Grammys
and many other awards. Her unique and stunning
singing ability still has a profound effect on many
listeners and has influenced many other singers.

Chapter 1

Love

Love can be a very complicated thing for adults to figure out and deal with. And it can get really messed up in the minds of young people, especially young girls. I like to think of love as a nurturing relationship where people are encouraged to grow and become a better person.

Think about the love you have for your mother and father. They don't always do what you want them to do or allow you to do everything that you want to do. Why? Because they care about you. They are willing to let you and your relationship with them experience some short-term unhappiness or pain in order for you to grow and become a better person down the road. Do you love them less because they don't let you have or do whatever you want? No, I didn't think so.

Love is not about satisfying your immediate needs. Little sisters, this is serious stuff here, so I'm going to say this loud and clear: If you have a male in your life who is only trying to satisfy your (and his) immediate needs, get out of that relationship! He doesn't love you because he isn't willing to allow you to grow and succeed.

Let me give you some warning signs about boys and their use of the word "love." Many times at your age the "L" word is thrown around without much thought or meaning behind it. When a boy tells you that it's okay to have sex with him because he can't live without you or because he wants to buy you things or because he wants to marry you one day, then he doesn't really love you. All that's happening here is that the boy and you are getting your immediate needs met. And this is not love.

I have found that for a person to really know how to love and how to be loved, she has to first learn to love herself. This means that you know and understand that your life has purpose and meaning. It also means that you have learned to respect yourself. So, any boy who is trying to disrespect you does not love you. He's actually harming you because he's hindering you from growing and succeeding.

Respect yourself and be strong. If you tell a boy that you don't want to have sex with him and he tells you that he won't love you unless you do, or that he wants to show how much he loves you by having sex, cut him loose as fast as you can! People who respect themselves and others also respect other people's answers. "No" means "No." If he doesn't respect or approve of your answer, then he is not worthy of your time and affection.

Little sisters, I want to talk with you about something that makes me mad and sad at the same time: young girls having babies. There are way too many of you out there who think that having a baby will give you the love that might be missing in your life. Well, this kind of thinking is just plain wrong.

Let's play the tape all the way forward and discuss this for a minute. You may think that by having a baby you will have something to nurture and take care of – and that you will feel love back. But remember, someone is going to have to change the baby's dirty diapers, provide the baby with food and clothing, get up at all hours of the night tending to the baby's needs, and take care of a million other responsibilities that go along with being a good parent. And that someone will be you.

Little sisters, babies need a lot – and I mean a tremendous amount – of time, attention, and love. Let's be straight here: You are far from ready to do all these things. Heck, some adults aren't even ready!

There are many practical reasons why you aren't ready to have a baby yet. For example, you'd have to quit school and get a full-time job to earn the money you'd need to support a baby. And you would need medical insurance to cover the baby's health costs. There are many other reasons like this that I could go on and on about.

Let's talk about another kind of reason. And that is, you are not yet capable of giving a baby real love. Why? If you haven't been loved in the right way or you don't love yourself, then you aren't capable of loving and caring for a baby. Little sisters, the fact is you can't give away something that you ain't got.

Finally, having a baby to satisfy your need for love is selfish, irresponsible, and wrong. When a young girl brings a child into the world, the baby is automatically starting out at a huge disadvantage. Real love is waiting until you are older, wiser, and in a position to give a child a chance to succeed. You should want your child to have a better chance of realizing his or her goals and dreams than you did, to learn and know more than you do, to have more than you have, and to be able to do better in life than you have. Now that's real love.

What Do You Think?

What is your definition of "real" love?

Has your definition of love changed after reading this chapter? How?

What are some warning signs that a boy really doesn't love you?

What does Ella Fitzgerald's quote at the beginning of the chapter tell you about real love?

_____

_____

_____

_____

_____

_____

_____

_____

_____

_____

_____

_____

_____

_____

_____

"I don't think of myself as a poor, deprived ghetto girl who made good. I think of myself as somebody who from an early age knew I was responsible for myself, and I had to make good."

Oprah Winfrey
Producer and Actress
(Born 1954)

Oprah Winfrey's unmarried parents separated soon after she was born, leaving her to be raised by her maternal grandmother. At age 6, she moved in with her mother, where Winfrey was sexually abused by male relatives and friends. At age 14, she went to live with her father. Winfrey credits him with saving her life. Today, she is the first African American to own her own TV studio. The multi-talented Winfrey is host of her own talk show, businesswoman, actress, owner of a movie production company, and generous contributor to many charities.

Chapter 2

Poverty

In today's world, you are bombarded with things like MTV and rap music, Britney Spears and Janet Jackson, tattoos and body piercing, earrings and other jewelry, DVD players and cell phones, and countless other material things that the media is marketing in order to get your money. Now, owning or trying to acquire some of these things is not necessarily bad. Where many young girls get messed up is in how they perceive having or not having all these things. Many young girls think that they are poor and live in poverty because they don't have enough of these things. But this kind of thinking about poverty or being poor couldn't be further from the truth.

There are two kinds of poverty. One form of poverty is not having your basic needs met: that means not having things like adequate shelter, food, clothing, or water. I grew up around dilapidated and rat-infested buildings and homes, cars that sometimes started and sometimes didn't, and school books that, if the school could afford enough of them, were outdated and falling apart. But, I had my basic needs met. And, more importantly, I had love from my family, a faith and trust in God, a belief in myself, and a motivation to succeed.

In other words, there was no "poverty of the spirit" in my life. This is another kind of poverty, and, if you suffer this kind, it will have the greatest impact on whether or not you will grow and succeed.

When I was your age, there were times when I thought as you probably do: that I was poor because I didn't have everything I wanted. But I've grown to learn that this is wrong thinking. Just because you don't have all the material things you desire doesn't mean you can't succeed. As long as you are rich in your belief in yourself and your internal power to succeed, you will never be poor.

So, instead of focusing on what you don't have, focus on the things that you do have. Realize that the wonderful relationships you have in your life with your family, good friends, community, church, school, and teachers are what will help you in your quest to reach your goals and dreams. It's been my experience that the girl who, on the outside, appears to have it all is usually the one who is the poorest in spirit. She's usually the person who doesn't think much of herself, isn't motivated to succeed, and is likely to fall for the first man who comes along offering to give her all sorts of good things. In the end, she won't learn how to get her real needs met.

I don't want you to be this girl. So, don't focus on what material things you don't have. Instead, take a look at how rich your relationships with God and others are. This is the measuring stick of whether or not you are rich or poor, and what will keep you from experiencing poverty of the spirit.

What Do You Think?

What does it mean to have a "poverty of the spirit"?
How is this different from the way most people
define poverty?

_____

_____

_____

_____

_____

_____

_____

_____

_____

_____

_____

_____

_____

Describe all the ways that you are "rich" in your life today.

_____

_____

_____

_____

_____

_____

_____

_____

_____

_____

_____

_____

_____

What does Oprah Winfrey's quote at the beginning of the chapter tell you about how to look at and handle poverty?

_____

_____

_____

_____

_____

_____

_____

_____

_____

_____

_____

_____

"If you are going to think black, be positive about it. Don't think down on it, or think it is something in your way. And this way, when you really do want to stretch out, and express how beautiful black is, everybody will hear you."

Leontyne Price
Opera Singer
(Born 1927)

Leontyne Price was the granddaughter of two Methodist ministers in Mississippi. She first began singing in the church choir. Her parents encouraged her musical talents at home. In 1957, Price sang in her first opera. She went on to become the first African American singer to become world famous in opera. Price won 20 Grammy Awards and the Presidential Medal of Freedom. She was always aware of her role as a pioneering African American in opera and worked hard against racial prejudice.

Chapter 3

Racism

In today's world, you see African American males and females in the news and on TV all the time. Oprah Winfrey is a major influence in today's culture, and she's a multibillionaire. Colin Powell is the Secretary of State and one of the most respected people in American politics. African American women have made their mark in business and education. Naomi Sims runs her own cosmetics and hair care company; Mary Frances Berry, a professor of history at the University of Pennsylvania, also heads the U.S. Commission on Civil Rights.

There are many actors and singers who are smashing successes in the movie and music industries. In addition to sports stars in football, basketball, and baseball, African Americans like Tiger Woods in golf and Venus and Serena Williams in tennis dominate sports that have traditionally not seen many African Americans participate. All in all, there are many successful African Americans who are easily visible for you to see.

When I was growing up, it was much different. African Americans in the public eye were few and far between. As a matter of fact, I didn't even see an African American in a schoolbook until I was in college. There were countless injustices involving racism that took place when I was your age that were very public and in my face. But I didn't let it deter me from striving for what I wanted in life.

It's important for you to know and understand that all people are different, even those within the African American culture. Sometimes it's hard to get along with people who are close to you, let alone others from different cultures. But if you want to succeed, you must learn to accept and get along with all people, regardless of the color of their skin or any other way that they are different from you.

The fact is that racism has harmed and suppressed African Americans for many, many years. But that doesn't mean you should let it overcome you today. It's important for you to strive to love and accept all people who are different from you. You must learn to embrace diversity, and instead of focusing just on a person's race or other ways he or she is different from you, make an effort to learn about and understand how you are similar. This kind of thinking and action will provide you with better friends, give you a healthier outlook on life, and, ultimately, give you a better chance to succeed.

I remember being in a job interview where the man doing the interviewing and hiring was white. He told me that from what he read in my resume – especially my educational experience and background – he had thought I was white. After we talked a while, he was very impressed with me and admitted that he had never worked with an African American before. He said he was willing to give it a try if I was. Now, instead of being offended or getting caught up in the stereotypes that this man had, and saying I didn't want the job, I looked at this as an opportunity for me to educate a person about the African American culture. It was a chance to break down some of the stereotypes that this person held. Over time, he was so impressed with who I was as a person and the work I did that he asked me and my husband to come over to his house for dinner. At that time, this was a big deal because African Americans weren't welcome in his neighborhood.

The point here, little sisters, is that there are many people in different cultures who are just like this man: uneducated about the African American culture but willing to learn more. Being uneducated about cultures doesn't automatically make people racists. Granted, those people are out there. However, I choose to believe that many people are simply ignorant – they just don't have the right information and don't know where to go to get it. I also believe that many people, once they are informed, become more understanding and accepting of differences.

Little sisters, I ask you to think and do the same. It's your responsibility to embrace those who do not understand our culture, to accept them as they are, and to look for opportunities to help people of other cultures learn about and come to understand what the African American culture is all about.

But remember, you can't give away what you haven't got. In order to help educate others and break stereotypes, it's up to you to learn more about your culture and where you came from. Doing this also makes you more capable of accepting and learning about others and their differences.

Open yourself up to others. Don't get stuck in the problems of racism. Instead, break out of the pack and be strong enough in yourself to understand that God wants us to love and accept each other – differences and all.

What Do You Think?

Why do you think it is important to accept differences in other people?

_____

_____

_____

_____

_____

_____

_____

_____

_____

_____

_____

_____

What are some things you would tell others to help educate them about your culture?

In Leontyne Price's quote at the beginning of the chapter, she talks of being "positive" about being an African American. Why do you think that is important?

_____

_____

_____

_____

_____

_____

_____

_____

_____

_____

_____

_____

_____

What are some ways you can be positive in your own life?

"I never thought that a lot of money or fine clothes - the finer things in life - would make you happy. My concept of happiness is to be filled in a spiritual sense."

Coretta Scott King
Civil Rights Activist
(Born 1957)

Born on a farm in Alabama, Coretta Scott King grew up picking cotton as a way to help her family survive. She was an intelligent and hard-working student who attended and graduated from college. While there, she met the civil rights activist Martin Luther King Jr., and they eventually married. When her husband was assassinated, Scott King stepped in to carry on her husband's dream of an America where all people had equal rights.

Chapter 4

Worthlessness

When I look around the world today for an example of people who feel worthless, I'm immediately drawn to the homeless – the people who live and sleep on the streets. These are people who are tired of trying and have given up. They have allowed a sense of emptiness and an overwhelming feeling of worthlessness to take over their hearts and minds.

Feelings of worthlessness can also happen to people in the ghetto. Many times, it can happen like this: A person tries to get a job to support his or her family but there simply aren't enough employment opportunities. Even if the person is able to find a job, it's usually one that doesn't pay enough to sustain a family. So, the person is forced to turn to welfare to help his or her family survive.

Having to go on welfare creates tremendous feelings of worthlessness in people. Why? Because when you have to depend on the government for food, housing, medical care, and other things, you have to abide by the government's rules. And who wants to grow up and live with someone telling you what food you can buy, where you can live, and what medical treatment you can receive? All this causes a lot of pain in people's hearts and minds.

What I want to tell you, little sisters, is that you will encounter times in your life when you feel worthless and empty. It may not be from having to go on welfare; it may be due to something else that happens in your life (breaking up with a boyfriend, doing poorly in school). What's important is that no matter what obstacle you encounter, you must always remember that your life has meaning. God gave all of us a purpose in life and it's up to you to take charge of your life.

What can you do to overcome feelings of worthlessness when they do come into your life? Some of the following can help:

- I believe one of the best ways to overcome feelings of worthlessness is to turn to faith and prayer. This will help you realize and know that God loves you and that you are special to

Him. Remember, God has a plan for you. Sometimes we just have to be patient until we learn what that plan is.

- Talk to others about your feelings. You can talk to a pastor, teacher, coach, school counselor, friend, family member. Don't be embarrassed to talk with others about these feelings because they have more than likely felt the same thing. They know what you're going through. And they can help you to work through these feelings so they don't stop you from growing and succeeding.

- Do things for others. Volunteer, serve the homeless, help an elderly neighbor, get involved in helping others through your church. There are a million things that you can do to help others! When you give your time and talents to others and get the focus off yourself, the feelings of worthlessness often disappear because you begin to see that your life has meaning. Try it. It really works!

What Do You Think?

Have you ever had bad feelings about yourself?
What do you think caused those feelings?

_____

_____

_____

_____

_____

_____

_____

_____

_____

_____

_____

_____

_____

What are some ways to overcome feelings of worthlessness? In what ways can you apply these to your life?

Ask an older relative (parent, grandparent, aunt, uncle) what he or she thinks Martin Luther King Jr. would have told you about how to overcome obstacles in your life. Write down the response here.

_____

_____

_____

_____

_____

_____

_____

_____

_____

_____

_____

_____

_____

_____

_____

_____

_____

"There is no obstacle in the path of young people who are poor or members of minority groups that hard work and preparation cannot cure."

Barbara Jordan
Lawyer, Educator, Congresswoman
(1936-1996)

Barbara Jordan was born in Texas during the time of segregation. While growing up, she experienced discrimination in many areas of her life. However, she didn't let this stop her. Jordan became a lawyer, educator, and politician who served in the U.S. House of Representatives from 1972 to 1978. She was the first black congresswoman to come from the Deep South. Jordan was widely admired for her great speaking abilities during many important political events, such as the Watergate impeachment hearings and the 1976 Democratic National Convention.

Chapter 5

The American Dream

I hear people, young and not so young, say that the "American dream," which put simply means working hard to succeed, doesn't exist or apply to African Americans. Well, little sisters, I'm here to tell you that this kind of thinking is wrong. Your goals and dreams can be realized just like anyone else's – and don't let anyone tell you otherwise.

As young African American girls, you will have obstacles pop up as you journey toward success. But this also is true for young people in any other culture from any other country. Obstacles don't discriminate.

I believe that America offers more opportunities than any other country in the world. Third World countries like those in Africa, Asia, and Latin America don't come near to offering the wonderful educational and job opportunities you have in America. However, from my experience, I believe that people in Third World countries do have solid family foundations and traditions and a strength and motivation to make their lives better. They are very focused on not letting obstacles get in their way.

Many young African American girls do not have this same focus and strength because, in reality, they haven't really struggled. You may think you have struggled or are struggling now. But real struggle can be seen from people in Third World countries who have to overcome barriers every day just to get adequate food, water, shelter, and clothing. They have nothing like welfare to fall back on when times get tough. Even welfare in America is a better alternative than what these people have to go through.

America has systems in place to support people in pursuit of their American dream. But you, little sisters, have to stay steadfast in your pursuit of success, just as your mothers, fathers, and forefathers did. If your ancestors didn't have visions of better lives, you wouldn't be here today.

The African American culture has survived and thrived due to the dreams of others before you.

Now, it's your responsibility to keep those dreams alive and continue to help our culture grow. You are the future of African American culture.

As young girls, it's natural to get frustrated or down when obstacle after obstacle gets in the way of your growth and success. When this happens – and it will – seek out those positive and caring people in your lives. Tell them how you're feeling and look to them for advice, encouragement, and inspiration.

When I think of the American dream, I will always think of Dr. Martian Luther King Jr. He had a vision that all girls and boys should be able to pursue their dreams and that they should be granted the opportunity to do so regardless of their race or culture. Dr. King died trying to make his vision a reality. So, if you have a desire to succeed, give it everything that you have. Look to Dr. King and others who have realized their dreams for inspiration. Dream, little sisters, and work hard to make those dreams come true!

What Do You Think?

After reading this chapter, what does real "struggle" mean to you?

_____

_____

_____

_____

_____

_____

_____

_____

_____

_____

_____

_____

_____

How are you going to achieve your goals and dreams?

_____

_____

_____

_____

_____

_____

_____

_____

_____

_____

_____

_____

_____

_____

Read Barbara Jordan's quote at the beginning of this chapter again. What kind of hard work and preparation can help you succeed?

"It's not the load that breaks you down, it's the way you carry it."

Lena Horne
Singer and Actress
(Born 1917)

Lena Horne began performing at the age of 6. At 16, she was forced to leave school to support her sick mother. She became a singer and dancer, performing in famous Harlem nightclubs. In 1938, Horne started a movie career and eventually became the first African American woman to sign a long-term movie contract with a Hollywood studio. In the 1950s, Horne was an outspoken foe of racial discrimination. This had a negative impact on her career, but she never wavered in her beliefs.

Chapter 6

Pressure

Pressure can come from many different sources: friends, school, family, yourself, and others. Pressure can be good for you (like the pressure you put on yourself to get good grades in school) and it also can be a bad, even destructive, force in your life (such as peer pressure to do drugs).

At your young age, bad pressure is all around you; it's almost impossible to escape it. There are pressures to be thin, pretty, accepted among your friends, have material things, drink, have sex, and so on. So, the first thing to understand and accept, little sisters, is that pressure, both good and bad, is a part of life.

What I want to say to you is this: Don't let the pressures that you experience overwhelm and dominate your life. Why? Because once you allow this to happen, they have tremendous power over you and your thoughts and actions. Ultimately, if you allow them to take over your life, you will begin to lose motivation to work hard to make your success a reality. When you give in to the pressures to drink, do drugs, or have sex, you are only hurting yourself. You are not respecting and loving yourself. And, you won't succeed.

Let's talk a bit, little sisters, about some ways that you can resist and overcome some of the bad pressures you'll face.

- Faith and prayer are some of the best ways to resist and overcome bad pressure. Sometimes you might not feel like talking to someone about the pressures that the girls and boys are putting on you. At these times, turn to God. Have a conversation with Him. Tell Him what's going on and ask Him for guidance. God will help if your faith and beliefs are strong.

- Ask someone you are close to and trust if he or she has been in a situation like the one you are experiencing. If so, ask that person how to handle the pressure and overcome it. It's up to you to seek these people out. They won't just magically appear when you need them.

- Remember that for every pressure or problem there are many solutions – both good and bad. There also are consequences for each one of those solutions. So, think carefully about each possible solution and make sure that whatever solution you choose is one that helps to make you successful.

- Many times, it helps just knowing that you're not alone. Keep in mind that whatever problem or pressure you are dealing with, there is or has been someone somewhere who has experienced the same thing – and who worked everything out successfully in the end. So, take comfort in knowing that you're not the only one experiencing problems and pressures.

- Seek out the counsel and advice of your elders, especially your grandmother or a caring and knowledgeable aunt. These people have a wealth of life experiences for you to draw from, and they want to share and help you. Just reach out to them for a helping hand!

What Do You Think?

What can happen when you give in to the pressures around you?

What are some of the bad pressures that you face in your own life today?

How can you overcome those pressures?

What does Lena Horne's quote at the beginning of
the chapter say to you about how to handle pressure?

"I pray hard, work hard, and leave the rest to God."

Florence Griffith Joyner
Olympic Sprinter
(1959-1998)

Florence Griffith Joyner grew up in Watts, a very poor section of Los Angeles, the seventh of eleven children. Determined to make something of herself, she rode the L.A. city buses for hours each way to get to school. Not only was she a good student, but she also was a great runner. In 1988, she set a world record in the 100-meter dash. Later that year, Griffith Joyner won three gold medals in the Olympics. After retiring from track, she was a member of the President's Council on Physical Fitness and worked tirelessly to help underprivileged children living in some of the worst neighborhoods in the country.

Chapter 7

Faith and Spirituality

It's impossible to go after and achieve your goals and dreams without a belief and faith in yourself. This faith and belief in yourself can be learned and nurtured by developing a faith in and having a relationship with God. And you learn all this from going to church.

I understand that you might think that church is boring and not as exciting as watching MTV or going to a concert. But you will have many wonderful experiences and meet so many wonderful people if you just show up and participate.

Let me tell you a little about some of the really neat things that I have found by going to church and having a relationship with God. When I was your age, church gave me another source to help me deal with my problems. There were always people around who were interested and willing to talk to me about solutions to the tough issues and problems I was experiencing. I've found that most people who belong to a church and attend services regularly are there to help others in need.

I also found wonderful role models outside my family whom I could talk to and spend time with. These people reached out to me and showed me that they cared about me as a person. They wanted to help me achieve my goals and dreams.

Learning to have a relationship with and faith in God is not always easy. By going to church and talking to the people there, I learned how to pray and talk to God. These people taught me how to have a relationship with God and the importance of faith in my life. I learned what a wonderful feeling you get about yourself when you help others. All of this (and more!) is waiting there for you, too. But first you have to suit up and show up!

Little sisters, people will sometimes disappoint you and let you down. This is when a relationship with God can have its greatest impact on your life. By having a good relationship with God, you'll develop a great sense of comfort and peace in knowing that you have another source to go to and depend on any time, any place when times are tough.

Having a relationship with God teaches you how to have faith. It not only gives you a faith in God, but also teaches you how to have faith in yourself. What you'll find is that the more you believe and have faith in God, the more faith and belief you'll have in your ability to reach your dreams and goals.

Have a relationship with your church. When all else fails and you hit rock bottom, you can always count on God, your church, and the people within. They can show you that faith allows you to go beyond what you think you can do. They can help you learn a sense of inner strength, provide you with the ability to see beyond the problems of today, and help you to know and believe that things will work out. Put simply, little sisters, faith gives you hope!

What Do You Think?

Why is your faith and having a relationship with God so important to your success?

What can you do to strengthen your faith and have a better relationship with God?

What does Florence Griffith Joyner's quote at the beginning of the chapter mean to you?

"The kind of beauty I want most is the hard-to-get kind that comes from within - strength, courage, dignity."

Ruby Dee
Actress
(Born 1924)

Growing up in Harlem, Ruby Dee developed an interest in the theater at a young age. In 1945, she graduated from college and began performing on Broadway and in film. Dee is also a published novelist, poet, and columnist. Throughout her life, Dee risked her career many times to speak out on civil rights and other political issues.

Chapter 8

Self-Esteem

Low self-esteem means that you don't feel good about yourself. It can also mean that you feel like you aren't worth anything or that your life has no meaning. It's a terrible feeling and one that can have many negative effects on your life. When you don't feel good about yourself, you become more open to giving in to the negative pressures and influences all around you.

The boys who are up to no good – and you know who I'm talking about – more easily prey upon girls who have low self-esteem. These kinds of boys will try to come around with phony offers of love. Let's be real here. They want one thing and one thing only from you: sex.

What scares me is that girls with low self-esteem only see a quick fix to feeling good. What they fail to realize is that the amount of time they might feel good is very, very short, and that the consequences of their actions often lead to tremendously harmful long-term problems. For example, for a quick fix of feeling good, you could end up pregnant or hooked on drugs and alcohol.

It's the same thing with girls joining gangs. Many of the young girls who join gangs feel like they are without love, attention, and affection. So they turn to a gang. Here they feel like they have a sense of family, belonging, and importance because they are part of something.

Little sisters, I'm here to tell you that a gang is not the way to get your needs met. All it will lead to is more pain, and it will ruin any chance that you have to grow and succeed.

When you have an inner strength, a good sense of who you are, and a thirst for making your life better, you are much less likely to give into negative influences like gangs, alcohol, drugs, and sex. You don't want or need the instant gratification that these things vainly try to offer you.

The way to improve how you feel about yourself and pump up your self-esteem is to have a healthy knowledge of all the issues that we've discussed in this book. In other words, you will feel better about yourself when you don't let things like poverty, racism, peer pressure, and feelings of worthlessness rule your life or have a negative influence on how you think and act. Being self-motivated, having faith in and a relationship with God and others in your church, and knowing and experiencing real love improves your self-esteem.

Don't take the shortcuts to feeling good, little sisters. All these shortcuts do is lead you away from the path of attaining what you want from life.

What Do You Think?

In what ways does feeling good about yourself have a positive effect on your life?

_____

_____

_____

_____

_____

_____

_____

_____

_____

_____

_____

What can you do that would help you have a
more positive outlook on yourself and your life?

What does Ruby Dee's quote at the beginning of the chapter say to you about what things are important to feeling good about yourself?

"Challenges make you discover things about yourself that you never really knew. They're what make the instrument stretch - what make you go beyond the norm."

Cicely Tyson
Model and Actress
(Born 1933)

Cicely Tyson was the daughter of immigrants and grew up in Harlem. She spent time working as a secretary and a model. Eventually, Tyson moved into acting on the stage and screen. She was nominated for an Academy Award and won two Emmy Awards for her acting. Tyson gave up the opportunity to appear in many more movies and TV shows because she chose to portray only strong, positive images of African American women.

Chapter 9

Loneliness

We were created to be with and around others. All of us need people – family and friends – to help us become happy, healthy, and successful human beings. One of the worst feelings is to feel like you're all alone in the world, that there's no one you can talk to or spend time with.

Many of you out there feel this way. But, little sisters, you don't have to feel alone if you don't want to. There are many things you can do to allow and bring others into your life to help fill it with joy and meaning. We'll talk about some ways you can do this in just a minute. First, let's discuss why many of you get to the point where you feel so alone.

I believe that there are two main reasons why many of you feel lonely today – you've isolated yourself from your family and friends or you have become caught up in material things. You might be experiencing one of these or both. Either way, the result is the same: a feeling of loneliness and emptiness.

I grew up playing jump rope and board games with my family and friends. Recently, I was having fun with my great nieces and they didn't know how to jump rope or how to play Monopoly, a traditional and popular board game. But, these girls were whizzes on how to use instant messaging and surf the Internet.

The point I'm making here is that many kids today create their own loneliness. How? By spending so much time by themselves watching TV, surfing the Net, instant messaging, and talking on cell phones. When you let these things dominate your time, you shut others out of your life, especially your family.

In order for you to grow and be successful, your family and others must be positive forces in your life and be actively involved in helping you. If you choose to shut them out, you'll just fade into your own little world that's filled with isolation and despair – and you won't grow.

The other reason kids are lonely is because they get caught up in accumulating things like the newest clothes, jewelry, cell phones, and many other things. One of the most powerful and consistent messages that our culture sends to kids – all kids – is that the purpose of life is to accumulate material things. Many kids think that a good and successful life is measured most by a person's material wealth. Little sisters, this is a myth – it couldn't be further from the truth. I believe that real wealth means that a person has a good heart and a strong mind, and is able to make good decisions and choices when faced with challenges and obstacles. As a matter of fact, some of the wealthiest people in terms of dollars are the loneliest and poorest in spirit.

Kids are meant to be part of a family. But the desire for material wealth can lead them to bad decisions and choices. Some kids turn to selling drugs or joining a gang to make fast money or as a quick way to get the things they want. What happens is that these kids stray from and lose their real family. They wrongly think that happiness is found in accumulating material things. Soon, these kids learn how mistaken this kind of thinking and behaving is, and they find themselves all alone with no one to turn to. And in the end, most of these kids are sucked into the negative elements in their environment – drugs and alcohol, sex and teen pregnancy, gangs and violence – as a way to escape the loneliness.

Little sisters, you need a loving and nurturing environment, one where people love you and care about you. This happens within your family, whether it's with your mom and dad and brothers or sisters, or with other people in your family like your grandmother, aunt, or cousins. The important point I'm making here is that you need to stay with your family to be successful.

When you create your own little world by shutting others out or by letting the accumulation of material wealth run your life, you end up developing a "loneliness of the spirit." This is one of the most demoralizing and terrible feelings that I know. It makes you feel like you're no good and that your life has no purpose, and it derails you from achieving your mission.

You need others to support and encourage you on your journey to success. Life's too hard sometimes to go it all alone. People close to you want to help you reach your goals and dreams.

How can you avoid or overcome loneliness? Let's go over some the ways.

- **Make it your priority to be around your family whenever possible.** Interact and talk with your parents, brothers and sisters, and other relatives. They are there to help you, and you can learn many life lessons from them.

- **Eat dinner with your family or a family member whenever possible.** I know that life is very busy for parents and kids, but make an effort to be there when family meals are served, even if it's just once a week. When life gets real busy, go ahead and ask a family member to eat a meal with you. During this time, you can listen, learn, and ask others how they have solved problems, grown, and succeeded.

- **Play and have fun with your friends and family.** Get off the phone and computer! Get away from the television! Spend time playing outside or play things like board games inside where you have to interact and talk with others. It's fun! Try it. You'll find yourself and your family and friends laughing and talking about some really neat things.

- **Go to and participate in your church.** Hang around after the services and get involved! Join groups for young people. There are lots of other kids at church who you can get to know. I know I've never felt lonely at church!

- **Get involved in community or neighborhood projects and activities.** There's always something going on in your neighborhood or community to help make it a better place to live. Get out there and participate! You'll meet lots of really neat young people.

- **Volunteer to help others.** For example, go visit the elderly. They'd love to talk with you! Or, go see sick kids in the hospital. They need people like you to help and encourage them. When you focus on finding ways to help others, you don't have time to be lonely.

What Do You Think?

What are two reasons many kids feel lonely? Do they apply to your life?

_____

_____

_____

_____

_____

_____

_____

_____

_____

_____

_____

_____

_____

What are some ways to overcome loneliness? How can you put them to work for you?

Ask a relative or a friend what he or she thinks Cicely Tyson's quote at the beginning of the chapter says about how to deal with loneliness. Write the response here.

"You may encounter many defeats, but you must not be defeated. In fact, it may be necessary to encounter the defeats, so you can know who you are, what you can rise from, how you can still come out of it."

Maya Angelou
Author and Poet
(Born 1928)

Maya Angelou was born in St. Louis to parents who divorced shortly after her birth. When she was 8, her mother's boyfriend raped her. She was so traumatized by the sexual assault that she refused to speak to anyone but her brother. Angelou and her brother were sent to live with their grandmother, who lived in a rural Arkansas town. After four years there, she started to speak to others again. Her life took many dramatic twists and turns, but she became a well-respected and world-famous poet, writer, and educator. Angelou continues to give her heart and soul to improving conditions for women in Third World countries, primarily in Africa. She has helped change the live of thousands less privileged.

Chapter 10

Pain and Pleasure

"I want what I want and I want it now!" Have you ever heard someone, maybe a friend or a brother or sister, say something like this? Have you ever said or thought something like this? Come on now… be honest. Little sisters, when I was your age, I used to have thoughts like this one. It's normal for younger people.

All of us, no matter our age, would prefer to get our wants and needs met as quickly as possible. No one likes to do without, suffer, or endure discomfort or pain any longer than he or she has to. But, a big part of reaching your goals and dreams involves learning that life isn't all about getting your wants and needs met instantly.

Many times in life you have to go through some discomfort, suffering, and pain in order to succeed. For example, if your goal is to graduate from high school and move on to college, you're going to have give up some things you really enjoy, like hanging out with friends all night long, so you can get your homework done. And, you're going to have to experience some discomfort and pain, like getting up early to get to school on time.

Life can be hard. I understand this from experience. But experience also has taught me that trying to instantly solve problems by avoiding or escaping discomfort and pain usually leads a person down a very unhealthy path. Let me explain this further by telling you a story about a friend of mine, Joelle, who I knew growing up in Chicago. Listen closely; she might sound like someone you know.

Joelle had a very difficult situation going on at home. Her stepfather was sexually abusing her. This caused Joelle great pain. The way she chose to deal with the problem and pain was to smoke marijuana. She thought doing this made her feel better. Soon, Joelle started hanging around boys and girls who liked to smoke marijuana. We didn't hang out much together after that because I wasn't into the drug scene. I knew where that kind of choice led – and it didn't lead to me reaching my goals and dreams.

Before long, Joelle had a boyfriend who was much older than she was. He supplied her with the all the marijuana she wanted, and she spent more and more time with him. Joelle started skipping school and doing whatever it took to please her boyfriend. She was hooked on drugs and was avoiding life by getting high.

As time went on, Joelle needed more and more marijuana to get high, but she didn't have any money to pay for her habit. So, she started having sex with her boyfriend to keep the supply coming. After a while, the marijuana didn't get her as high as she wanted so she started doing cocaine. My dear little sisters, do I need to go any further? I am sure you can guess what happened: Joelle got pregnant and hooked on drugs.

She ended up having three babies. Sometimes when I would drive down the street, I would see Joelle looking for men to have sex with so that she could get money to buy drugs. You see, her boyfriend was long gone. All three of her children had different fathers.

Joelle's life started down the path of ruin the minute she chose not to face the pain at home. Instead of dealing with the pain head-on by choosing to talk to a teacher or counselor about what was happening, Joelle chose to instantly avoid and escape her problems by getting high.

Yes, telling a teacher or counselor would have been very hard, and it may have caused even more problems at home. But, little sisters, life is filled with tough decisions and choices. Don't be afraid of confronting your problems head-on and dealing with the pain. Take comfort in knowing that most of the discomfort and pain you'll experience will be short-lived. When you face your problems head on, the pain doesn't last as long. Avoiding and escaping your problems just makes them worse and more complicated to solve in the long run. Just remember what happened to Joelle.

I know that all of this is hard for you to under-stand and do when you're all mixed up in a problem. But trust me: Avoiding or escaping the discomfort and pain that some problems bring simply leads to more problems.

People spend years going to school to become educated. It's a great sacrifice to work hard in school and get good grades. As time passes, you will learn and experience many new things. All this helps to prepare you for adulthood. When I finished high school, I sacrificed getting a job and being able to buy myself nice things right away – like some of my friends did – so that I could fur-ther my education by going to college. You see, little sisters, studying, working hard, and doing well in college prepares you for an even better job. Education is one of the keys to success!

I chose to delay having all the material things my girlfriends had because I wanted to get a good job – one that required a college degree. I chose to set my goals and dreams high. I wanted to feel that I had accomplished something big. In order to achieve all this, I had to sacrifice and delay my immediate wants and desires. This was the only way for me to succeed.

When you go to work every day, you have to give up some of the things you'd rather be doing – like watching TV or going shopping. But, when you show up and work hard, you get paid. For some people, a steady paycheck is all they need to keep them coming back to a job. But I wanted more. I wanted a job that stimulated and challenged me. Don't get me wrong; I wanted to get paid, but I also wanted to enjoy what I did at work.

My point here, little sisters, is to set your goals and dreams high when it comes to school and work. Finish your education so that you have many job options and opportunities. It's nice to get a paycheck but it's even sweeter to look forward to the challenge that a job you enjoy can bring.

Little sisters, remember that life is full of challenges and obstacles to overcome. Remember that
all problems have solutions and that some solutions require us to endure some discomfort and
pain. But in the end, the wonderful feelings that
come from overcoming a problem far outweigh
any short-term discomfort or pain.

One final thing that I want you to always be
aware of: Your forefathers suffered as slaves. They
suffered tremendously to make the world a better
place for you and all African Americans. So, as an
African American female, you are genetically put
together to survive, endure crisis, and solve problems. And, you are responsible for continuing to
make the world a better place for the next genera-
tion of African Americans.

What Do You Think?

What is the difference between what you *need* and what you *want*?

Why are school and education so important to success?

_____

_____

_____

_____

_____

_____

_____

_____

_____

_____

_____

_____

_____

_____

_____

How can you make getting an education a top priority in your life?

Ask a teacher to read Maya Angelou's quote at the beginning of the chapter and tell you what it means to him or her. Write the response here.

_____

_____

_____

_____

_____

_____

_____

_____

_____

_____

_____

_____

_____

_____

"I always wanted to be somebody. If I made it, it's half because I was game enough to take a lot of punishment along the way and half because there were a lot of people who cared enough to help me."

Althea Gibson
Tennis Player
(1927-2003)

Althea Gibson grew up in the streets of Harlem; her family was getting by on welfare checks. She struggled in school, but was a fantastic athlete and excelled in many sports. When Gibson was young, African Americans were barred from playing tennis on the public courts in New York. A wealthy African American realized Gibson's talent and helped her get private lessons and the court time she needed to get better. Tennis helped instill discipline in Gibson, and she went on to attend and graduate from college. Later, she entered women's professional tennis. She overcame the tremendous prejudice and racism that dominated tennis in her time and was the first African American to win the Wimbledon and U.S. Open singles championships.

Chapter 11

Role Models

There will be times in your young life when you will feel down and troubled. You will encounter problems at home and school that seem so messed up and overwhelming that you think nothing can be done to solve or overcome them. These are the times when you need a helping hand – someone to bounce your thoughts and feelings off of and to help advise you on the best path to take. This is when a "role model" can best guide you.

Role models are people who are older and wiser than you. They are people whom you look up to and respect. You admire how they live their life in a positive manner. You trust them with your thoughts and feelings, enjoy being around them, and know that they care about you and have nothing but your best interests in mind.

Role models come in all shapes and sizes. They can be a parent, teacher, grandmother, aunt, church member, coach, or a relative of one of your friends. You can have one role model or many. As a matter of fact, the more positive role models you have in your life, the better off you'll be!

I found my most powerful role models in my family. This is the first place you should look for good role models. My mother was the absolute bomb! She was not well educated but she was very wise and could tackle very difficult problems effectively. She taught me about all sorts of positive things I needed to know in order to reach my goals and dreams. Much of what she taught me you can't learn in school. She taught me about common sense, God, prayer, sharing, caring, loving, and most importantly, how to give to others. She taught me to believe in myself and how to overcome obstacles with diligence and prayer.

My mother had nine children. She had very little material wealth because she sacrificed buying things for herself so that her children could have the things they needed to succeed. Mom never drank, smoked, or used a curse word. She made sure that our family went to church on Sundays, and that we had a home-cooked meal afterwards. Mom always put herself second, sacrificing her time and strength to make sure that her husband and children were healthy and happy. She was a wonderful role model!

It's tough being a mom and even tougher when you want to be a great mom like my mother strived to be. Always remember that raising a child is not just about you. It's about providing a child with the best possible environment to grow and learn, and teaching him or her the inner strengths needed to be successful in life.

When I was growing up, another one of my role models was my older sister. I remember one time when I was going on a date to a very fancy restaurant. I was very nervous about what to wear and how to use all the different utensils that come with your food. I talked to my sister about all this and she took the time to teach me what to do. She taught me how to look cultured. She taught me about etiquette. And the dinner turned out great! My sister was the person I went to for advice about dating and boys. I knew she loved and cared about me and would answer my questions and help me out in any way she could.

So you see, different role models can provide you with insight and advice, based on their experiences, on how to best tackle some of life's issues and problems.

Role models can have many positive influences on your life. They can teach you important life skills and life lessons. Here are just a few things that a good role model can help you with:

- They can teach you important life skills that will help you succeed in school, work, and relationships with family and friends.

- They can teach you about values and morals and how to instill these in your life.

- They can teach you that all people have challenges and problems, and that there is more than one way to tackle them.

- They can help you find positive solutions to problems.

- They can teach you about real love, not the kind of mistaken love that many young girls think that having a baby will bring.

- They can help teach you about faith in God and the importance of having a relationship with Him.

- They can help teach you how to pray, and they can pray for you, too.

What Do You Think?

Who are some of your role models?

Why are they good role models for you?

_____

_____

_____

_____

_____

_____

_____

_____

_____

_____

_____

_____

_____

What are some of the ways your role models have had a positive impact on your life?

Ask one of your role models to read Althea
Gibson's quote at the beginning of the chapter
and tell you what it means to him or her. Write
the response here.

"I look at a stream and see myself: a native South African, flowing irresistibly over hard obstacles until they become smooth and, one day, disappear."

Miriam Makeba
African Singer and Activist
(Born 1932)

A native of South Africa, Miriam Makeba was an outspoken critic of the horrible conditions, racism, and prejudice the black people of her country faced in the 1960s. Because of her political views, the South African government forced Makeba to leave the country. She moved to the United States. While there, Makeba became the first African singer and performer to gain a worldwide following, and she played a big role in introducing the sounds and rhythms of traditional African music to the West.

Makeba continued her fight for racial freedom in her home country, and in the late 1980s, returned to her homeland as a free South African.

Chapter 12

Purpose

Little sisters, I truly believe that God has put each and every one of you on this earth for a reason. He has a plan for you. You have been blessed with unique qualities and talents to help you fulfill His plan. It's up to you to discover what these qualities and talents are and to put them to good use during your lifetime. This is what I mean when I say that your life has a purpose. Each of your lives has meaning and is valuable.
Figuring out your life's purpose doesn't always come easy. I've learned that it takes time and unfolds differently for each person. This means that some of you will find your purpose early on in life. For others, it might take quite a bit longer.

Discovering God's plan for your life is something that can't be forced or rushed. You have to be patient – and that's hard! But with each day that passes, you grow and mature and learn more about yourself and others. As you grow and learn, you become stronger and more determined, and more is revealed to you about your uniqueness – your purpose.

Knowing that your life has a purpose means that it's your responsibility not to sell yourself short. So, when your boyfriend asks for sex or a friend tries to get you to drink alcohol or do drugs, you must understand that this is not what God intended for you to do with your life. It's important to fill your life with positive people and positive things so that you are empowered to find out what's unique about you.

Some of you might be blessed and destined to become doctors, lawyers, or actresses. Some might become great teachers, terrific listeners, or have a delightful singing voice. Some of you will have unique talents in fixing hair or cooking. My point here is that everyone has a unique purpose and one purpose isn't better than any other. What's important is that you work as hard as you can to capitalize on your strengths and find what you enjoy.

As I said earlier, finding your special purpose may be a hard thing to figure out. How can you do it? Well, let me share with you some ways that worked for me. They might also help you on your journey.

- **Religion and Faith.** Having a relationship with God is a great way to help you answer your calling. One of the best ways to improve your relationship with God is through prayer. Talk with God and ask Him to help you be patient and to guide you toward your purpose. He will be there if you sincerely seek Him out and trust that He will reveal His plans for you. Little sisters, I have found that prayer is very important to reaching your goals and dreams and to finding your purpose. Remember, you can never pray too much!

- **Education.** I can't stress how important school and education are in your life. Education can help you overcome lots of barriers and open up to you many new opportunities that you once thought were impossible to obtain. School can give you a glimpse of what profession you might like to pursue. In school, you will be exposed to some subjects that you find you really enjoy and find intriguing. These are usually the ones that will motivate you to keep on learning.

  Education also can help you learn what some of your limits are. What does this mean? Let me explain. Have you ever heard the phrase, "You can be whatever you want to be?" Little sisters, this isn't always true. Everyone is not cut out to be a doctor, lawyer, teacher, mom, or accountant. Each one of these vocations requires different types of talents, skills, and personalities. If you are not equipped with the right stuff, you more than likely won't succeed and you'll be unhappy. Sometimes, it's simply not the right match for you. My point here is to take school seriously and be open to a wide variety of learning opportunities. Over time, with the help of others and God, you'll land right where you're supposed to be.

- **Confidence.** Be confident in yourself and the fact that you were meant for a greater purpose. Take pride in accomplishing the things that you do well – school, work, sports, having lots of friends, and so on. Make an effort to do even better at the things you do well and improve in the areas where you don't do so well. Simply put, never stop trying to improve yourself. And, most importantly, don't believe that you or your situation can't change – it can as long as you believe that it can happen!

- **Helping Others.** One very important way to find your purpose is to unselfishly give of yourself to others. Volunteer to help out at church, nursing homes, or hospitals. There are so many people and organizations out there who desperately need people like you to assist them in their missions. When you make it a priority to give your time and talents to others, you find out a lot about yourself. It helps you feel good about yourself and about the meaning and purpose of your life.

- **Loving Others.** Loving others is sometimes a hard thing to do, especially if you have been let down or hurt. But, little sisters, never stop loving. The rewards are too great to pass up, even though you might fear the times when love hurts. In order to truly know who you are and discover your life's purpose, you have to first love yourself. This will enable you to love others. People who know that you genuinely trust and love them want to help you. They want you to be happy and are willing to do whatever it takes to help you find your purpose.

What Do You Think?

What are some of your gifts and talents?

In what ways have you put your gifts to use in your life?

What are some ways you can go about finding
your purpose?

Ask a parent or older relative (your grandparent, aunt, uncle) to read Miriam Makeba's quote at the beginning of the chapter and tell you what it means to him or her. Write the response here.

Chapter 13

Listen Up, Little Sisters

Some of you out there feel hopeless every now and again, and some of you feel like there is no hope at all. At times, tough issues like poverty, racism, loneliness, and others can overpower you and have a negative influence on how you think, feel, and act. This clouds your vision for becoming a better person and succeeding.

Little sisters, I don't want you to ever lose hope. Once you do, you stop learning and moving forward. Hope keeps you striving to become a better person and to achieve what you want in life.

One of the best ways to keep hope alive is having the right information about the issues we have discussed in this book. When you're armed with the correct information, you gain a more positive outlook on your life. Things don't look as bleak as you once thought. This leads to a willingness to learn how to overcome your problems and develop a more positive attitude. In the end, you're better able to accept life on life's terms, and you aren't as likely to let these potential negative influences affect you.

Little sisters, one day you will turn into young ladies. Then you will become women, and many of you will even become mothers. Just remember to be patient; don't be in any rush. All your goals and dreams can be realized as long as you stay strong and keep your eyes squarely focused on the prizes ahead. Always remember that no matter how bad your problem or situation might be, you are important in God's eyes. He has plans for you and your life, and your life has meaning!